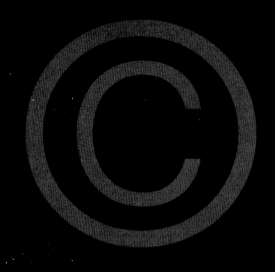

First published in the United States of America by
HailesArt, LLC
P.O. Box 71443,
Salt Lake City, UT 84171.

June 2010

www.hailesart.com
www.bchailes.com

Printed in China

ISBN 10   0-9825994-1-2
ISBN 13   9780982599419

10 9 8 7 6 5 4 3 2 1

THE

DANCE QUOTE

BOOK

WITH ARTWORK BY B.C. HAILES

HAILESARTS

Intro

People dance in many styles and for different reasons. Dance can be used to express emotion or tell a story. It can be a means of social interaction or of spiritual ritual. Dance can be for the performance of virtuoso techniques or as a competition to prove one's skill. But foremost, dance is a celebration of life. One cannot fully appreciate what it means to dance without experiencing it. The joy of feeling the blood quicken in the veins, the blurred sensation of movement as the world swirls past the vision, the tension of muscles as one rises above the pull of gravity; these indescribable pleasures cannot be felt by observing, but by doing. These are the reasons dancers work to perfect their craft.

Every dancer must have discipline. Dancers are crafted by years of sweat and pain, and a resultant sense of pride and dedication is inevitable. Dancers forge their bodies to be strong or soft, large or small, sinuous or delicate. Some refine their bodies for quick, bright movement, while others are powerful and bold. Not only are physical sacrifices endured, but also those of a personal or social nature. For their countless hours of practice, there is no doubt that they experience certain solitude, ever working to train and shape themselves into an ideal tool. They strive each day to make the very best of God's gift to them. Dancers will push their bodies to the limits of physical capability as they tune them to become fine instruments of expression. The living sculpture of the human body may only briefly shine during a period of youthful energy, but within the warm, brilliant lights of the stage, they will be forever remembered.

The dancers introduced herein and the words of those who have lived within the studio walls where these bodies have been honed have been brought together with Hailes' sensitive drawings to touch the hearts and minds of all those who exist on the other side of the lights. And it is the hope of all involved in the creation of this project that the translation will be clear and the reader will not only see, but also experience the dancer within. May the light that falls on these pages find the reader with an understanding and appreciation of the artist's purpose.

_Sandra W. Emile
Dancer, Choreographer
& Artistic Director of the
Cache Valley Civic Ballet

Introduction

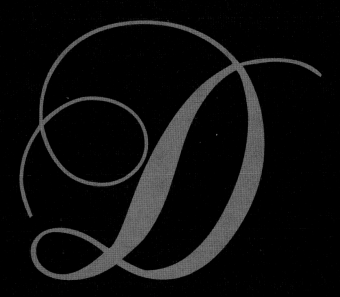

Dance: To move one's body rhythmically, to leap or skip about, to move nimbly or quickly, to perform or take part in, to use prescribed or improvised steps and gestures, to show joy, excitement or emotion.

*D*ancing is the loftiest, the most moving, the most beautiful of the arts, because it is no mere translation or abstraction from life; it is life itself.

_Henry Havelock Ellis

B.C. HAIES

*D*ance is movement, and movement is life.

_Ludmilla Chiriaeff

plate 4   (left) | "energy" | pencil on bristol board

To dance is to be out of yourself--larger, more beautiful, more powerful. This is power, it is glory on earth and it is yours for the taking.

_Agnes De Mille

plate 5   (right) | "freedom" | pencil on bristol board

B.C. HAILES

*D*ance is music made visible.

_George Balanchine

plate 6   (left) | "excitement" | pencil on bristol board

To dance, above all, is to enter into the motions of life. It is an action, a movement, a process. The dance of life is not so much a metaphor as a fact; to dance is to know oneself alone and to celebrate it.

Sherman Paul

plate 7   (right) | "spirit" | pencil on bristol board

$\mathscr{I}$ don't want people who want to dance, I want people who have to dance.

_George Balanchine

plate 8   (left) | "feeling" | ink on bristol board

To dance is to give oneself up to the rhythms of all life.

_Dr. Maya V. Patel

plate 9   (pg 28-29) | "sisterhood" | pencil on bristol board
plate 10   (right) | "allure I" | pencil/ink on bristol board

*D*ance is your pulse, your heartbeat, your breathing. It's the rhythm of your life. It's the expression in time and movement, in happiness, joy, sadness and envy.

_Jacques D'Ambroise

plate 11   (left) | "pulse" | pencil on bristol board

*I*t is an art that imprints on the soul. It is with you every moment. Even after you give it up. It is with you every moment of your day and night. It is an art that expresses itself in how you walk, how you eat, how you make love, and how you do nothing. It is the art of the body, and as long as a dancer possesses a body, he or she feels the call of expression in dancers' terms.

Shirley MacLaine

plate 12   (right) | "dedication" | pencil on bristol board

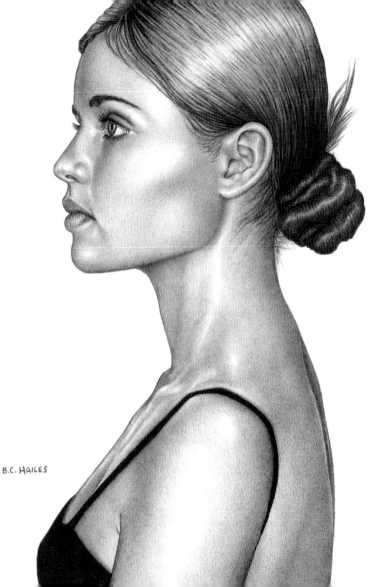

B.C. HAILES

B.C. HAILES

To watch us dance is to hear our hearts speak.

Derrick "Suwaima" Davis

plate 13   (left) | "grace" | pencil on bristol board

I see dance being used as communication between body and soul, to express what it finds too deep for words.

_Ruth St. Denis

plate 14   (right) | "allure II" | pencil on bristol board

Art: The quality, production, expression, or realm, according to
aesthetic principles, of what is beautiful, appealing, or of more than
ordinary significance.

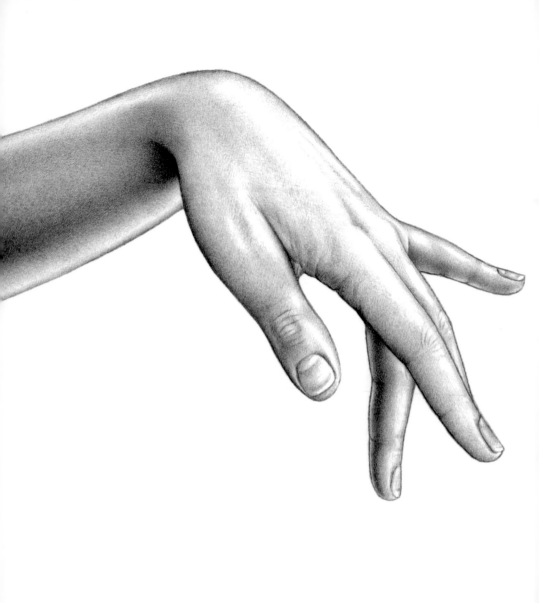

*I*n all its forms, dance is an art, a celebration of life; it is movement and line, a careful discipline of muscle and bone, a fine balance of passion and spirit. It is inspiration.

_B.C. Hailes

Artists lead unglamorous daily lives of discipline and routine, but their work is full of passion. Each has a vision and feels responsibility to that vision.

_Merryl Brockway

plate 17   (left) | "remembrance" | pencil/ink on bristol board

*G*reat artists are people who find ways to be themselves in their art. Any sort of pretension induces mediocrity in art and life alike.

_Margot Fonteyn

plate 18   (right) | "**preparation**" | pencil on bristol board

B.C. HAILES

O body swayed to music, O brightening glance, How can we know the dancer from the dance?

_William Butler Yeats

plate 19   (left) | "balance" | pencil on bristol board

The essence of all art is to have pleasure in giving pleasure.

_Mikhail Baryshnikov

plate 20   (right) | "happiness" | pencil on bristol board

*W*hy do I dance? Why do I breathe?

_Unknown

plate 21   (left) | "life" | pencil on bristol board

*I*t's the heart afraid of breaking that never learns to dance.

_Bette Midler

plate 22   (right) | "reflection" | pencil on bristol board

No artist is ahead of his time. He is his time; it is just that others are behind the times.

_Martha Graham

plate 23   (left) | "touch" | mixed media/digital

Art

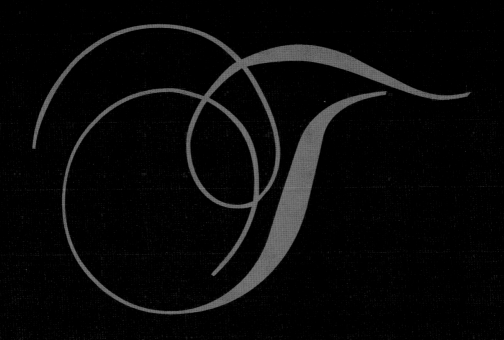

Technique: The manner and ability with which a dancer, athlete, or the like employs the technical skills of a particular art or field of endeavor. Also, the method of performance; way of accomplishing and projecting personal charm or appeal.

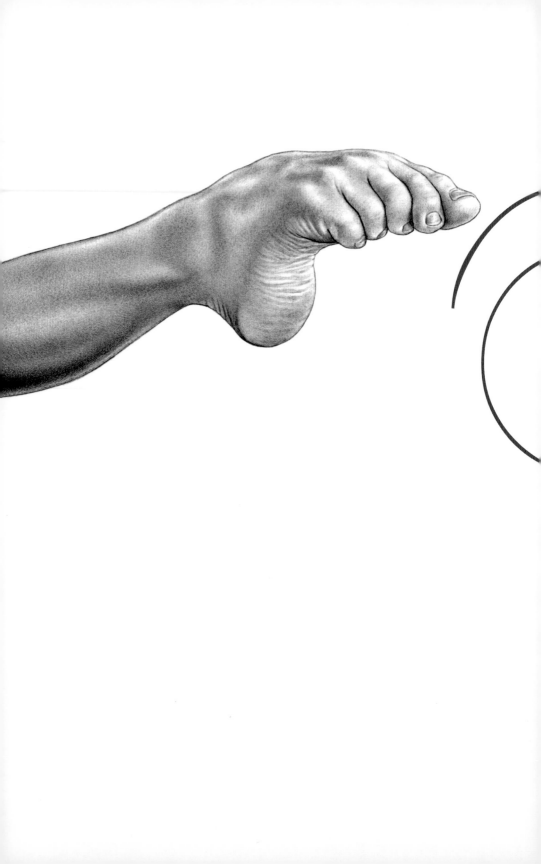

Technique

*R*eal dancing happens on the space of a stage and to be aware of that space--its flexibility, its rules, its relationship to the audience... One goes out on stage with a well-prepared technique, a knowledge of how to present that technique in its most refined form. But beyond that, what counts is the ability to be free on the stage to dance... I know now that style is what gives blood and color to the bones of the piece, the technique.

_Mikhail Barishnikov

plate 24   (pg 62) | "point" | pencil on bristol board
plate 25   (right) | "position" | pencil on bristol board

B.C. HAILES

*I*n life as in dance, grace glides on blistered feet.

_*Alice Abrams*

plate 26   (left) | "gliding" | pencil on bristol board

*G*reat dancers are not great because of their technique; they are great because of their passion.

_Martha Graham

plate 27   (right) | "charm" | ink on bristol board

*I*t is not so much upon the number of exercises, as the care with which they are done, that progress and skill depend.

_*Auguste Bournonville*

plate 28   (left) | "partnership" | pencil on bristol board

Technique--bodily control must be mastered only because the body must not stand in the way of the soul's expression.

_La Meri

plate 29   (right) | "practice" | pencil on bristol board

B.C. HAILES

*I*f their feet aren't in the right place, at least their hearts are.

Christian M. Chensvold

plate 30   (left) | "training" | pencil/ink on bristol board

*W*hen I dance, I cannot judge, I cannot hate, I cannot separate myself from life. I can only be joyful and whole. That is why I dance.

_Hans Bos

plate 31   (right) | "charisma" | ink on bristol board

B.C. HAILES

*A*ll the dancer's gestures are signs of things, and the dance called rational, because it aptly signifies and displays something over and above the pleasure of the senses.

_St. Augustine

𝓘 do not try to dance better than anyone else. I only try to dance better than myself.

_Mikhail Baryshnikov

plate 34   (right) | "progression" | pencil on bristol board

$\mathcal{B}$allet's image of perfection is fashioned amid a milieu of wracked bodies, fevered imaginations, Balkan intrigue and sulfurous hatreds where anything is likely, and dancers know it.

_Shana Alexander

plate 35   (left) | "intrigue" | pencil on bristol board

History: Dance does not often leave behind clearly identifiable physical artifacts that last over millennia, and it is not possible to say when dance became part of human culture. But dance has certainly been an important part of ceremony, rituals, celebrations and entertainment since before the birth of the earliest human civilizations.

History

*D*ancing is at once rational and healthful: it gives animals spirit; it is the natural amusement of young people, and such it has been from the days of Moses.

_William Cobbett

plate 36   (pg 88-89) | "belly dance" | pencil on bristol board
plate 37   (right) | "promise" | prisma pencil on carnival paper

Human beings, vegetables, or comic dust, we all dance to a mysterious tune intoned in the distance by an invisible player.

Albert Einstein

*H*ence it is from the representation of things spoken by means of posture and gesture that the whole of the art of dance has been elaborated.

_Plato

R.C. HAILES

*A*ll the art of living lies in a fine mingling of letting go and holding on.

Henry Havelock Ellis

plate 41   (left) | "poise" | pencil on bristol board

*T*he truest expression of a people is in its dance and in its music. Bodies never lie.

_Agnes de Mille

To everything there is a season...and a time to dance.

_Ecclesiastes 3:1-8

plate 44   (left) | "potential" | pencil on bristol board

History

Purpose: The reason for which something exists or is done, made or used. An intended or desired result; end; aim; goal. Determination; resoluteness.

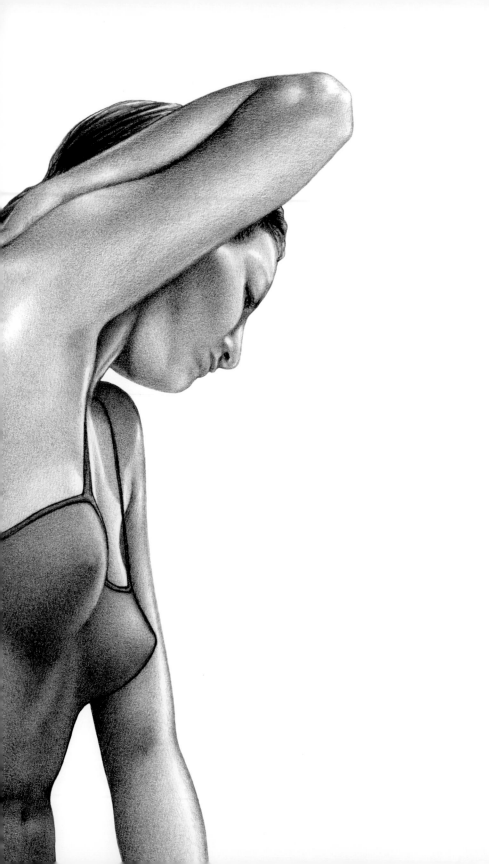

*T*here is vitality, a life force, an energy, a quickening, that is translated through you into action, and because there is only one of you in all time, this expression is unique. And if you block it, it will never exist through any other medium and will be lost.

_Martha Graham

plate 45   (pg 108) | "stretching" | pencil on bristol board
plate 46   (right) | "delicacy" | prisma pencil on carnival paper

B.C. HAILES

*D*ance is so important in the world. It needs no language. Our bodies speak a language of their own.

Ibrahim Farrah

plate 47   (left) | "splendor" | pencil on bristol board

*T*here is a bit of insanity in dancing that does everybody a great deal of good.

_Edwin Denby

plate 48   (right) | "muscle" | ink on bristol board

*D*ancing can reveal all the mystery that music conceals.

_*Charles Baudelaire*

plate 49   (left) | "mystery" | ink on bristol board

The music gets stuck in your mind and the dance is in your heart and the whole scene is engraved on your soul. You can fly.

_Nicholas Hope

plate 50   (right) | "flight" | pencil on bristol board

There are shortcuts to happiness, and dancing is one
of them.

_Vicki Baum

plate 51   (left) | "lights" | pencil/ink on bristol board

Purpose

Beauty: The quality present in a thing or person that gives intense pleasure or deep satisfaction to the mind. An individually pleasing quality; grace; charm.

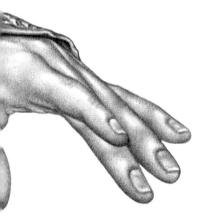

$\mathscr{B}$eauty is the sole ambition, the exclusive goal of taste.

_*Charles Baudelaire*

plate 52   (pg 124-125) | "beauty" | pencil on bristol board
plate 53   (right) | "appeal" | pencil on bristol board

B.C. HAILES

Every beauty which is seen here below by persons of perception resembles more than anything else that celestial source from which we all are come.

_Michelangelo

plate 54 (pg 128-129) | "shining" | prisma pencil on carnival paper
plate 55 (left) | "repose" | pencil on bristol board

*B*eauty in things exists in the mind which contemplates them.

_David Hume

B.C. HAILES

$\mathcal{D}$ance is a delicate balance between inhibition and expression.

_Unknown

plate 58   (left) | "scorpion" | pencil on bristol paper

Beauty

Conclusion: The end or close; final part.

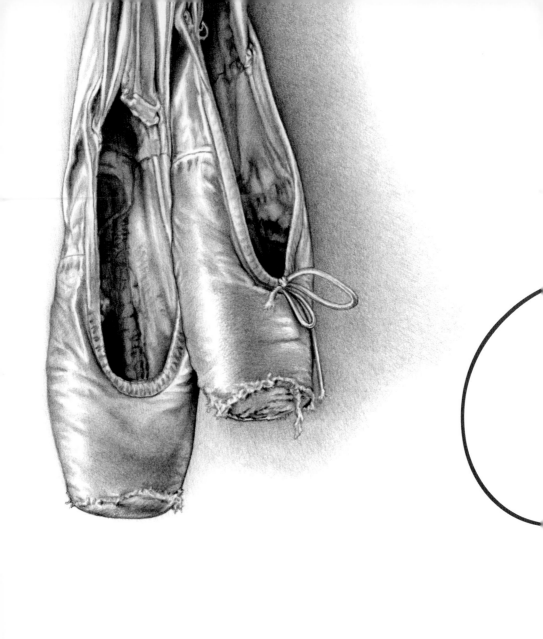

B.C. HAILES

*D*ance isn't something that can be explained in words; it has to be danced.

_Paige Arden

To those of us with real understanding, dancing is the only pure art form.

_Charles M. Schulz

plate 62   (left) | "attraction" | pencil on bristol board

$\mathcal{I}$ saw in the fugitive beauty of a dancer's gesture a symbol of life. It was achieved at the cost of unending effort but, with all the forces of gravity against it, a fleeting poise in mid-air, a lovely attitude worthy to be made immortal in a bas-relief, it was lost as soon as it was gained and there remained no more than the memory of an exquisite emotion. So life, lived variously and largely, becomes a work of art only when brought to its beautiful conclusion and is reduced to nothingness in the moment when it arrives at perfection.

_W. Somerset Maugham

plate 63   (right) | "expression" | pencil on bristol paper

*D*ance is like life, it exists as you're flitting through it, and when it's over, it's done.

_Jerome Robbins

plate 64   (left) | "dip" | pencil on bristol board
plate 65   (pg 152-153) | "ecstacy" | pencil on bristol board

Conclusion

Acknowledgments: Expressions of appreciation.

models

MICHELLE ARMSTRONG
Dancer/Ballet Centre

SILVER BARKES
Dancer/Ballet West

MEAGAN B. CHADWICK
Model/Utah State University

CHELSEA ERICKSON
Dancer/Ballroom Utah

REBECCA B. ERICKSON
Dancer/Cache Valley Civic Ballet

FELICIA FULLER
Dancer/Ballet Centre

TODD HANSEN
Dancer/Ballroom Utah

JEFF F. HERBIG
Dancer/Ballet West

CLINT KNAPP
Dancer/Utah State University

TARYN D. LAVERY
Dancer/Cache Valley Civic Ballet

TAWNA LE WARD
Dancer/Utah State University

MANDY MCLACHLAN
Dancer/Ballroom Utah

LUSIANO PASILLAS
Dancer/Ballet Centre

KYNASTON SCHULTZ
Dancer/Central West Ballet

STEFANY SEITZ
Dancer/Ballet Centre

JOSEY SILVA
Dancer/Ballet West

JILL D. STEWART
Model/Utah State University

LARISSA SWENSEN
Dancer/Ballet Centre

MARK A. WEBER
Dancer/Ballroom Utah

Also a Special Thanks to:

ARTISTS OF **BALLET WEST**   WWW.BALLETWEST.ORG

ARTISTS OF **CACHE VALLEY CIVIC BALLET**   WWW.CVCBALLET.ORG

ARTISTS OF **CENTRAL WEST BALLET**   WWW.CWBALLET.ORG

ARTISTS OF **BALLET CENTRE**   WWW.WRIGHTWAYENTERPRISES.COM

ARTISTS OF **BALLROOM UTAH**   WWW.BALLROOMUTAH.COM

ARTISTS OF **UTAH STATE UNIVERSITY**   WWW.USU.EDU/BALLROOM

quotes

(in alphabetical order)

Brian C. Hailes attended classes at the Academy of Art University in San Francisco, and received his BFA degree from Utah State University. Before his graduation, he also spent a full semester to study in New York City, interning at the Society of Illustrators.

Hailes has worked as a freelance illustrator, designer, and commission artist for over a decade, and has received numerous awards for his art from all across the country, including Winner in the USPS National Stamp Design Competition, the Best of Show Award in the Brigham City Statewide Art Competition, and in 2002, he won the L. Ron Hubbard Illustrators of the Future Contest out of Hollywood.

Hailes has written and illustrated two of his own graphic novel series, entitled "Dragon's Gait" and "Devil's Triangle" and has finished a new series called "Continuum" to be published in 2010 by Arcana Studios. He currently resides in Salt Lake City where he works full time writing, designing and illustrating.